BASEBALL

by
Jane Duden

CRESTWOOD HOUSE
New York

Maxwell Macmillan Canada
Toronto

Maxwell Macmillan International
New York Oxford Singapore Sydney

Library of Congress Cataloging-in-Publication Data
Duden, Jane
  Baseball / by Jane Duden.—1st ed.
  p. cm. — (Sportslines)
  Summary: A collection of facts and trivia about baseball.
  ISBN 0-89686-625-4
  1. Baseball—United States—Miscellanea—Juvenile literature. [1. Baseball—Miscellanea.]
  I. Title. II. Series.
  GV867.5.D83   1991
  796.357'0973—dc20   91-7365
                                                              CIP
                                                               AC

Photo Credits
Cover: AP—Wide World Photos
National Baseball Library, Cooperstown, N.Y. : 4, 7, 9, 10, 11, 13, 14, 15, 19, 20, 23, 25,
   27, 29, 31, 32, 33, 35, 36, 37, 39, 43, 45
UPI: 17, 21, 26
AP—Wide World Photos: 18, 30
New York *Daily News*: 22
Bob Bartosz: 28
TV Sports Mailbag: 36 (bottom)

CRESTWOOD HOUSE

Macmillan Publishing Company   Maxwell Macmillan Canada, Inc.
866 Third Avenue   1200 Eglinton Avenue East
New York, NY 10022   Suite 200
                                Don Mills, Ontario M3C 3N1

Macmillan Publishing Company is part of the Maxwell Communication Group of Companies.

Produced by Flying Fish Studio

Printed in the United States of America

First edition

10 9 8 7 6 5 4 3 2 1

Contents

Members of the New York City Knickerbockers. Alexander Cartwright is in the center of the rear row.

Inside Baseball

Discover why baseball is America's national sport! Turn the page for scores, stats and stories that will put you in the stands. Read about baseball's greatest moments from the earliest innings till now. Get to know the all-time stars. Enjoy personal bests, records smashed and unforgettable moments. *Sportslines* covers all the bases!

Who Invented Baseball?

No one "invented" baseball. It grew out of an English game called rounders. But Alexander Cartwright, a New York City bank clerk, wrote baseball's first rules. His team, the New York City Knickerbockers, played the first game under his new rules on June 19, 1846. Other teams were soon formed to compete with Cartwright's Knickerbockers.

Cartwright later caught the gold fever and headed west in a covered wagon. All along the way, Cartwright taught baseball to travelers, soldiers, saloon keepers, miners and even Indians. He spread the game around the country. His travels took him—and the game of baseball—to Hawaii for many happy years. His death in 1872, at age 72, was scarcely noticed outside of Hawaii. It wasn't until 1939 that Cartwright received official recognition as the father of modern baseball.

The Cooperstown Myth

You may have heard that Abner Doubleday invented baseball. That's a myth. So how did he get the credit for inventing baseball? The story started in 1907 when a group of men decided that baseball should be 100 percent American. They did not want it to be linked with the English game of rounders. So they made up a legend about Doubleday founding baseball in Cooperstown, New York, in 1839. The tale was based on a letter written by a very old man who'd gone to school with Abner Doubleday. The man thought he recalled a day in 1839 when Abner showed his friends how to play a game with a ball and bases.

In 1939 the major leagues made grand plans for the 100th year of baseball. The "centennial" would be in Cooperstown, even though the Doubleday story was being questioned. Cooperstown got the legend, the celebration and a famous museum—the Baseball Hall of Fame. But Alexander Cartwright's grandson sent diaries and clippings to the Hall of Fame organizers. These writings convinced the museum's founders of Cartwright's importance. So they put Cartwright in the new Hall of Fame and left Doubleday out. And, in a gentle mark of recognition, Babe Ruth placed flowers on Cartwright's grave.

The Leagues

"Major leagues" is the term for all the teams of the American and National leagues combined. They are often called the big leagues, the bigs, or the majors. Here's how it all began.

Baseball's National League (NL) began in 1876. Organizers were tired of the scandals and cheating that were common in the old National Association. William A. Hulbert was a businessman and a Chicago White Stockings fan. He called for a new league. He wrote its constitution. And he won the support of the big eastern teams—Philadelphia, Boston, Hartford and New York. The National League grew to 12 teams and flourished until 1899. Then four teams were dropped. Those four quickly linked up with an outlaw league and formed the American League (AL). Teams in the National League at this time were Pittsburgh, Philadelphia, Brooklyn, St. Louis, Boston, Chicago, New York and Cincinnati. The NL stayed that way until 1953.

The American League opened play in 1901 as an eight-team league. Charter members were Chicago, Boston, Detroit, Philadelphia, Baltimore, Washington, Cleveland and

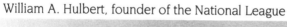

William A. Hulbert, founder of the National League

Milwaukee. St. Louis replaced Milwaukee in 1903. The teams stayed in the same cities until 1954.

The years since have brought many changes. Some teams have moved to other cities. The leagues expanded as new franchises were awarded and new teams formed. Today's National League has 12 teams and will expand to 14 teams in 1992. The American League has 14 teams. Baseball is still growing!

Owning Up

Joseph Borden threw the first no-hit game in the major leagues on June 28, 1875, as Philadelphia beat Chicago, 4–0. Borden didn't get credit for his feat until years later. Back when Borden pitched, baseball had a reputation as a low-class game. There were scandals and cheating. For that reason, Borden pitched under the name of Nedrob ("Borden" spelled backward). No one believed he was the first no-hit pitcher until after his death in 1929!

A Good Deal

Some old-time baseball teams made unusual trades. In 1890 a Canton pitcher named Denton True Young was sold to Cleveland for a suit of clothes. This suited Young fine. It was a good trade for Cleveland too. He came to be known as Cy Young. Why? In Canton the pitcher warmed up by throwing against a wooden outfield fence. His fastballs did so much damage that someone said the fence looked "like a cyclone hit it." A sportswriter heard the remark and dubbed him "Cy."

In 23 seasons in Cleveland, St. Louis and Boston, Cy

Young set pitching records that may never be broken. He holds the mark for most wins (511), complete games (756), and innings pitched (7,356). The game has not forgotten him. In 1955, shortly after he died, major league baseball's award

Cy Young

for the best pitcher was named in his honor. Since 1967 the yearly Cy Young Award goes to the best all-around pitcher in each league—American and National. The award is given by the Baseball Writers Association of America.

Top Card

To baseball-card collectors, Hall of Famer Honus Wagner is the biggest name of all. Playing for the Pittsburgh Pirates, he was the finest shortstop of his time. Wagner was also a model of clean living during his playing days (1897–1917). He demanded that a tobacco company's baseball card of himself be withdrawn from the market. He did not want to be linked with smoking. The card had only limited distribution and is therefore a collector's item. Today the 1909 Twentieth Century Tobacco card of Honus Wagner is worth more money than any other card. One of these rare cards was sold in 1989 for $115,000. It is worth as much as $400,000 in mint condition! You can see a Honus Wagner card in the Metropolitan Museum of Art in New York City.

A Honus Wagner
baseball card

Southpaw

Why are left-handed pitchers called southpaws? In most ballparks home plate is in the western corner of the diamond. (That way batters don't have to face into the setting afternoon sun.) When a lefty is on the mound, therefore, his pitching arm is on the *south* side of his body.

What a Relief!

The Chicago Cubs beat the Brooklyn Dodgers, 4–3, on June 17, 1915, but it took 19 innings to do it! Pitcher Washington "Zip" Zabel relieved for the Cubs with two outs in the first inning. Zip didn't know it then, but he would make the longest relief appearance in major-league history.

White Sox Become Black Sox

A small boy tagged after his hero, "Shoeless" Joe Jackson, as he left the grand-jury room. "Say it ain't so, Joe," he pleaded. "Say it ain't so." But to the horror of Jackson's teammates—and all of America—it was. Eight Chicago White

The 1919 Chicago White Sox

Sox players, including Shoeless Joe, had been caught in "the most gigantic sporting swindle" in history. They had made a deal with the nation's leading gamblers to lose the 1919 World Series to the underdog Cincinnati Reds. The 1919 White Sox became known as the Black Sox. The eight players were never found guilty in the courts. But they were banned from base-ball for life. Their story is remembered in the recent film *Field of Dreams*.

Changing the Game

Some important changes came to baseball in 1920. The spitball was banned. Officials thought this would clean up the game and increase hitting. (A few pitchers were still allowed to throw spitters until the ends of their careers.) The Bill Doak fielder's glove was introduced in this year. Unlike the old pancake glove, it had a natural pocket with leather laces to adjust the size. The bigger mitt and webbed pocket improved fielding.

Pricey Writing

While still in the minor leagues, he bought a pair of new spikes. But they hurt his feet. In the sixth inning, Joe Jackson took off the pinching shoes and played the outfield in his socks. The other players kidded him. The talented player became known as Shoeless Joe.

Today Shoeless Joe Jackson's signature sells for as much as $1,000. That's partly because he was at the center of the 1919 "Black Sox" scandal. It's also because samples of his handwriting are tough to find. Joe didn't know how to write and seldom picked up a pen.

Lou Gehrig

The Iron Horse

New York Yankee first baseman Wally Pipp had a headache on June 2, 1925. He asked for the day off. A rookie, 22-year-old Lou Gehrig, took Pipp's place. For the next 2,130 games, Lou Gehrig was never out of the Yankee lineup. He didn't leave it until May 2, 1939. A muscle and spinal disease known as ALS (amyotrophic lateral sclerosis) forced him to retire. The disease is now commonly known as Lou Gehrig's disease. Lou set a major-league record that still stands for most home runs with the bases full: 23. For his powerful hitting and record-breaking 2,130 consecutive games played, he was called the Iron Horse of the Yankees. He was voted into the Baseball Hall of Fame in 1939.

13

The Babe

More has been written about Babe Ruth than about any other American sports figure. Babe Ruth was born George Herman Ruth. One story says he was called George until his first professional game. Jack Dunn, manager of the minor-league Baltimore Orioles, led Ruth onto the playing field. A veteran teammate called, "Here comes Jack with his newest babe." From that day on, George Ruth was Babe Ruth.

Babe Ruth watches one of his 714 homers fly over the fence.

Babe entered the majors in 1914 as a pitcher with the Boston Red Sox. But he was too good a hitter to remain a pitcher. He proved it when he was sold to the Yankees as an outfielder. When he connected just right, the crack of the bat thrilled fans. Babe would watch the ball as it sailed for the seats. Then he would break into his home-run trot, on legs that seemed too spindly for his top-heavy body. It doesn't matter that Henry Aaron broke Ruth's career record of 714 homers. Never mind that Roger Maris, playing in more games, holds the single-season record for four-baggers with 61, one more than Ruth's best. The Babe is still considered the greatest home-run hitter of all time.

The Battling Georgia Peach

Others could hit the ball farther, run faster, field better, throw better. But no one scared rival pitchers, catchers and fielders more than Ty Cobb. Born in Georgia (the Peach State),

Ty Cobb

Ty was called the Battling Georgia Peach. He looked for every way to win. He trained endlessly. He hunted with weighted boots all winter to keep his legs strong. He practiced sliding into base until his legs were raw. He often filed his spikes before the games. Usually his legs were covered with scars, cuts and bruises. But it paid off. Those legs stole a record 892 bases. Ty stole 96 bases in one season! He got into many fights and had few friends, but Ty is one of only two players ever to get more than 4,000 career hits. He finished with an awesome total of 4,191 hits in 24 seasons with the Detroit Tigers (1905–26) and Philadelphia Athletics (1927–28). This record held for over 50 years, until Pete Rose broke it in 1985. Tyrus Raymond Cobb received the most votes in the first Baseball Hall of Fame election in 1936.

The Reds Did It First

Cincinnati gave baseball several firsts. In 1869 the city became the home of baseball's first all-professional team. (In 1876 the Red Stockings became the Redlegs, or Reds.) The home opening game in Cincinnati starts each National League season. The Reds were one of the first franchised teams to play at night (May 24, 1935, against Philadelphia at Crosley Field). They were first to travel by air. And they played in the first televised game (August 26, 1939, in Brooklyn).

That's No Bull

The bullpen is an area next to the playing field, usually alongside the foul lines. Relief pitchers and other substitutes warm up in this area. No one knows for sure why baseball uses the word "bullpen." But there are guesses. Some say pitchers

16

used to warm up somewhere out in a pasture. As far back as 1877, "bullpen" referred to a roped-off part of the outfield. This area was used for standing room. Still others say the word can be traced to Bull Durham tobacco signs. These signs were posted on the fences of many ballparks in the early 1900s. The signs pictured a giant bull. In many parks relief pitchers warmed up in front of the bull. What's *your* idea for the origin of baseball's bullpen?

What a Rookie!

Boston Red Sox rookie Ted Williams hit the first of his career homers on April 23, 1939. Williams went on to have one of the greatest rookie seasons in history. He clubbed 31 homers, scored 131 runs, drove in a league-leading 145 runs and batted .327. He hit .406 for the Red Sox in 1941. No other player has hit .400 since then! On September 26, 1960, the Kid closed out the last season of his career. In his final at-bat he sent a huge home run over Fenway's right-field fence. That farewell homer was the 521st of his career.

Ted Williams

TRIPLE-CROWN WILLIAMS TRIPLE-CROWN WILLIAMS TRIPLE-CROWN ? ? ??

Joe DiMaggio

The Yankee Clipper

On May 15, 1941, Joe DiMaggio began a unique trip through the baseball record books. On that day the New York Yankee outfielder began his famous batting streak. Day after day he punished pitchers with at least one hit in every game he played. On June 29 he broke George Sisler's American League record of 41 straight games. Three days later he toppled Wee Willie Keeler's 44-game major-league record. The end finally came on July 17 in Cleveland. Two brilliant plays by Cleveland third baseman Ken Keltner stopped the Yankee Clipper. After 56 games, the famous streak was over.

Yogi-isms

Yogi Berra was the squat, square catcher who played with the New York Yankees during their dynasty years. It was an awesome stretch, from 1947 to 1963. He set records for games played, at-bats, hits and singles. He played in 30 games in a row without an error. During his Hall of Fame career, Yogi Berra was known as a star catcher. His 313 career home runs set the record for catchers until Johnny Bench broke it in 1980. Yogi was a Most Valuable Player (MVP) three times. He appeared in a record 75 World Series games. But Yogi is also known for his funny, fractured sayings. They're known as Yogi-isms: "It ain't over until it's over." "You can see a lot just by observing." "We made too many wrong mistakes." "Baseball is 90 percent mental; the other half is physical." (That's when writers remarked, "Yogi may think fine, but he can't add.") His outstanding baseball skills and colorful talk made Yogi Berra a well-known and beloved character.

Yogi Berra

A Pioneer

It was tough for Jackie Robinson to stay cool on the playing field. Fans shouted racial insults. Opposing players jeered at him from the dugouts. He was not welcomed by his teammates. Runners slid with their shoe spikes aimed at his legs. Jackie Robinson had been carefully picked by Dodger owner Branch Rickey as the man who would shatter baseball's color barrier. Rickey wanted a ballplayer "with guts enough *not* to fight back." As the 1947 season unfolded, Jackie's courage and skill showed that it was wrong to judge people by their skin color. By midseason, he had won the respect of his teammates. They stuck up for Jackie when other teams taunted him. The Dodgers won the National League pennant that season. Jackie batted .297 and stole 29 bases. And the first black player to make it to the major leagues was named Rookie of the Year!

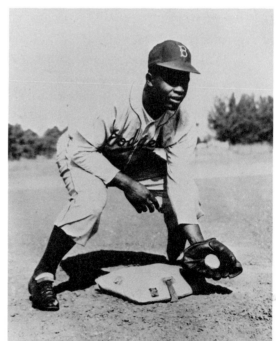

Jackie Robinson

Let's Hear It for the Fans!

In 1948 Joe Early, a night watchman, wrote to Cleveland Indians owner Bill Veeck. Why are players always honored? Why not a fan now and then? Bill Veeck was famous for his publicity stunts. So he had a special night for Joe Early. And what a night! Joe received an outhouse, a backfiring Model T and some weird animals. He also got a Ford convertible, luggage, a refrigerator, a washing machine, a watch, a stereo and clothes. What's more, Cleveland took its first pennant in 28 years.

Willie Mays

Say Hey!

During his 1951 rookie season with the New York Giants, Willie Mays sometimes forgot the names of his new team-mates. He'd say, "Uh, Say Hey." Willie Mays became the "Say Hey Kid." He played center field with dazzle. He was also one of the top sluggers of his era. Mays walloped 660 home runs in 22 seasons. He is third on the all-time list, behind Hank Aaron (755) and Babe Ruth (714). Willie topped them with 338 stolen bases. He was elected to the Hall of Fame in 1979, the first year he was eligible. When asked to name the best player he'd ever seen, Mays was honest. "I was," he said. He got no arguments about that!

Farewell, Babe

Yankee Stadium was called "the house that Ruth built." The happy-go-lucky, home-run–hitting Bambino drew crowds from the day the Yankees moved into their brand-new stadium in 1923. He hit the stadium's first home run. Twenty-five years later, on June 13, 1948, fans came to Silver Anniversary Day at Yankee Stadium. On that day they also came to honor one of the greatest of all baseball players—Babe Ruth. The Babe, his voice raspy from throat cancer, was cheered by over 64,000 fans. His number, 3, was retired. His uniform was sent to Cooperstown. Two months later, millions mourned the death of baseball's best-loved player, Babe Ruth.

Babe Ruth at Yankee Stadium the night his number was retired

Mickey Mantle

Tape-Measure Homer Hitter

It was April 17, 1953. New York Yankee Mickey Mantle hit a pitch in Washington's Griffith Stadium. The ball soared far, but it was no ordinary home run. A Yankee employee whipped out a tape measure and tracked the ball down. The ball had traveled an estimated 565 feet. It was baseball's first tape-measure homer! It was not the only time Mickey Mantle's hits called for tape measures.

No one ever hit a fair ball out of Yankee Stadium. But Mickey Mantle came close when he hit a 600-foot drive in 1962. Mickey said it was the hardest ball he'd ever hit. Everywhere Mickey played, he hit legendary homers. In the 1960 World Series, he became the first player to homer over the right-center wall in Pittsburgh's Forbes Field. His power hits in major-league stadiums earned him a reputation as the Commerce Comet!

Hitless

Jackie Robinson broke baseball's color barrier in 1947. On May 12, 1955, Sam "Toothpick" Jones of the Chicago Cubs performed another first. He became the first black to pitch a hitless game in the major leagues. His 4–0 win over the Pittsburgh Pirates was also the first no-hitter in Wrigley Field in 38 years.

El Bazooka

He once caught a fly 420 feet from home and threw out a runner who had tagged at third. No wonder players referred to Roberto Clemente's arm as El Bazooka! His style was unique both on and off the field. Because the number of letters in his full name—Roberto Clemente Walker—was 21, he chose 21 for his uniform number. Clemente played right field with the Pittsburgh Pirates from 1955 to 1972. He won 12 Gold Gloves. He hit .317 with four batting titles and exactly 3,000 hits. There's no telling how much farther baseball's first

Roberto Clemente

Latin superstar would have gone if his career hadn't ended abruptly at age 38. Roberto Clemente was killed in a plane crash while delivering emergency supplies to Nicaraguan earthquake victims on December 31, 1972.

Yogi Berra hugs Don Larsen after he pitched the only perfect game in World Series history.

One for the Record Books

On the mound at Yankee Stadium in the 1956 World Series, Don Larsen earned himself a special throne in baseball's Hall of Fame. He pitched a no-hit, no-run game in which not a single opposing batter reached first base. It would stand alone as the only perfect game in World Series history. The Yanks took the series lead three games to two, leaving the Dodgers and everyone else thunderstruck. Even Don Larsen was in a daze. His catcher, Yogi Berra, broke the spell when he ran onto the mound to leap full tilt at the big guy. That's how they made their way toward the Yankee bench, Larsen carrying Berra. It was one of the most fabulous World Series games ever!

Mets Moments

During their first season, the New York Mets team was the laughingstock of baseball. In 1962, the Mets' Marv Throneberry hit a triple. But he was called out for failing to touch first base. Manager Casey Stengel wanted to protest the call. A Met coach stopped him. "Don't bother," the coach said. "Marv missed second base too." In 1964 things began to change. A new stadium, Shea, was built in Queens, New York. The Mets surpassed the Yankees as the area's favorite team. In 1969, after seven years of play, the New York Mets won the World Series.

Fans and players celebrate the Mets winning the 1969 World Series.

Charlie Hustle

Pete Rose was just a Cincinnati Reds rookie back in 1963. New York Yankee greats Mickey Mantle and Whitey Ford saw him in spring training. Pete was gung-ho. He ran from the dugout to his position at second base. He ran from the on-deck circle to the plate. He ran to first base even when he drew a walk. One of the Yankees said, "Look at Charlie Hustle." The name stuck, and Pete Rose lived up to it.

Rose was a hometown hero for 16 seasons with the Reds. He was Rookie of the Year in 1963, Most Valuable Player in 1973, and World Series MVP in 1975. Pete got more hits than any other switch hitter in history. On September 29, 1977, Pete tied Ty Cobb's record of nine seasons with 200 or more hits. In 1981, at the age of 40, he broke Stan Musial's record (3,631) for the most hits in the National League. In 1989 Pete Rose, manager of the Cincinnati Reds, was banned from baseball, accused of illegal sports betting.

Pete Rose

28

Sandy Koufax

All in a Day's Work

L.A. Dodgers lefty Sandy Koufax pitched no-hitters in 1962 and 1963. He did it again in 1964 to tie Bob Feller's career record for most hitless games. On September 9, 1965, he pitched his fourth no-hitter in four years. Sandy Koufax was the first in baseball history to pitch four no-hitters. That's not all! His 1–0 victory over the Chicago Cubs happened to be a perfect game—no rival player reached first base. It was the eighth perfect game in baseball history.

Silencing the Bats

Pitching for the St. Louis Cardinals, Bob Gibson hurled his fifth shutout in a row on June 26, 1968. He beat the Pittsburgh Pirates, 3–0. He raised his scoreless streak to 48 innings. He was just 10-2/3 under Don Drysdale's existing record of six consecutive shutouts and 58 scoreless innings.

Gibson never spoke to players on opposing teams. He once explained, "I don't like any of you, and I don't want to get to know you because I might like you." It must have helped his pitching. On his way to winning the Cy Young Award, Gibson pitched 13 shutouts. He won 22 games and wound up with a 1.12 Earned Run Average (ERA)—the best in baseball since 1914 and the fourth best in history.

Bob Gibson

Stan the Man

Stan Musial became eligible for the Hall of Fame in 1969. Of course he was a top choice. Stan was one of the most feared hitters of his time. He was known as Stan the Man, plain and simple. The three-time MVP played with the St. Louis Cardinals from 1941 until 1963. Stan walloped 3,630 hits, making him fourth on the all-time list. He follows Pete Rose, Ty Cobb and Henry Aaron.

Hank Aaron breaks
Babe Ruth's
home-run record.

The Swing That Made History

The 1974 season had Atlanta Braves fans on the edges of their seats. It began with the Braves playing in Cincinnati on April 4. In his first turn at bat, the Braves' Henry "Hank" Aaron hit a sinking fastball over the fence. That hit tied Babe Ruth's cherished record of 714 home runs. Four days later in Atlanta, at exactly 9:07 P.M., Hank Aaron slugged a fastball pitched by Los Angeles Dodger Al Downing. The ball sailed past 52,780 yelling fans who had come to see history. The announcer screamed, "It's 715! It's out of here!" That hit was heard around the baseball world!

Writing in the Record Books

New York Yankee Reggie Jackson turned the 1977 World Series into a one-man show. He hit three straight homers and a total of five in the series. The only other man to hit three homers in a single World Series game was the legendary Babe

31

Reggie Jackson

Ruth. No one—not even Ruth—ever hit five homers in a single series. That power show earned Reggie Jackson the MVP award for the 1977 World Series against the Los Angeles Dodgers.

Hits at the Hall of Fame

What are the three most popular items in the Baseball Hall of Fame in Cooperstown, New York? Curator Ted Spencer has the answer. The original painting of three umpires by Norman Rockwell is one big hit. A continuously running videotape of Abbott and Costello doing the comedy routine "Who's on First?" is another. The third is Kansas City Royals infielder George Brett's controversial pine-tar bat. (Brett had hit a homer with that bat. Later in the game, the bat was discovered to have pine tar on the grip. Pine tar is sticky—helping the batter's grip and control—and its use on bats is illegal.)

What a Steal!

In 1977 Cardinal speedster Lou Brock stole a base that stole the show. He broke Ty Cobb's modern base-stealing record of 892. During the 1979 season, Brock got his 3,000th hit. That got him an invitation to the White House to meet President Carter. Just hours before his White House visit, Brock stole his 938th base. That gave him more steals than anybody in baseball history—and plenty to talk about with President Carter!

Lou Brock steals another base.

Mascots for Luck

On July 30, 1982, the Atlanta Braves flirted with Lady Luck. They removed their mascot, Chief Noc-A-Homa, and his tepee from the left-field area. This made more room for fans who wanted to see the first-place Braves. Did removing their mascot have anything to do with the Braves losing 19 of their next 21 games? Only after the tepee was brought back did the Braves regain first place.

Taking Licks

The only athletes to have been honored on a U.S. postage stamp are three golfers, two football players and four baseball players. The baseball players are Jackie Robinson (1982), Babe Ruth (1983), Roberto Clemente (1984) and Lou Gehrig (1989).

Big Bazooka Bucks

In 1952 a Mickey Mantle baseball card would have cost about a penny—part of a 5-cent package with four other cards and a stick of Bazooka bubble gum. Today that card would sell for about $8,900. When baseball cards were first issued in 1886, they weren't valuable at all. They came free in packages of cigarettes and chewing tobacco. Now baseball cards are a serious investment for collectors of all ages. Although only older mint-condition cards bring the top prices, some newer cards can be worth big bucks. A Bo Jackson card from 1987, for example, can be worth $20. Prices go up every year.

It's Outta Here!

Kansas City Royals rookie Bo Jackson hit his first major-league homer off Seattle's Mike Moore on September 14, 1986. It was no ordinary blast. The ball was the longest homer ever hit at Royals Stadium! It traveled an estimated 475 feet and helped the Royals win, 10–3.

Catcher Hits It Big

Who was the only major-league catcher to play in four different decades? He first played for the Boston Red Sox in 1969 in their minor-league system. He became a regular in

1972, when he was named American League Rookie of the Year. In 1989, playing for the Chicago White Sox, he broke Yogi Berra's American League record for homers by a catcher when he hit number 306. That player, still playing for the White Sox in the 1990s, is Carlton Fisk.

From Gang Leader to Home-Run Champ

Kevin Mitchell was once an inner-city gang leader. But then he figured it out. He said, "A shootout—you may *be* history. A home run—you can *make* history. Even if you strike out, you at least get another chance." The third baseman for the San Francisco Giants was the National League's 1989 MVP and home-run champ.

Baseball's Fastest Pitcher?

That might be Nolan Ryan of the Texas Rangers. He was clocked at 100.9 miles per hour in 1974 when he pitched for the California Angels. Nolan Ryan didn't think much about baseball records when he started pitching. But his 100.9-mph fastball has nabbed him some big ones. He's the all-time major-league leader in no-hitters and career strikeouts. On August 22, 1989, Ryan fanned Oakland's Rickey Henderson for his 5,000th career strikeout. It was the strikeout king's sixth 300-strikeout season!

Nolan Ryan

Ken Griffey Sr. (*left*) and
Ken Griffey Jr. (*right*)

Like Father, Like Son

In 1989 Seattle Mariner Ken Griffey Jr. and his dad, Ken Sr., of the Cincinnati Reds, became the first father and son to play in the major leagues at the same time. A broken bone in Ken Jr.'s little finger kept him out of 25 games. But the young outfielder still had a great rookie season. He batted .264 with 16 home runs, 61 runs batted in and 16 stolen bases. In 1990 father and son became teammates on the Mariners.

Who's Short Now?

Scouts once said that 5-foot-8 Kirby Puckett was too short to play in the big leagues. Kirby showed them. The Minnesota Twins outfielder has played in four All-Star games. Between 1985 and 1990 he had more hits (1,078) than any other major leaguer! In 1987 Kirby batted .332 with 28 homers, and the Twins won the World Series.

Kirby Puckett

Whaddya Say, Jose?

Jose Canseco said it himself. "Some sluggers just hit home runs. I murder the ball." And he does. In Minnesota's Hubert H. Humphrey Metrodome, he hit a ball that flew 457 feet, nearly reaching the unreachable second deck. His home run in Game 4 of the league championship series in Toronto went at least 540 feet.

Jose plays for the Oakland Athletics. He was the American League MVP in October 1988 after becoming the first player to hit 40 homers and steal 40 bases in a season—and the only member of baseball's 40–40 club!

Jose Canseco

Lockout

It looked as if there might be no baseball in 1990. The outlook was gloomy when team owners and players could not agree on a labor contract. The owners locked the gates to training camps, leaving players with no place to practice. They hoped that the lockout would make the players settle for a smaller share of the money earned by ticket and broadcasting sales. In mid-March, the owners and players reached an agreement. Training camps opened. Spring training began. And fans could watch their favorite sport again.

Cecil's 51st

Nobody had hit 50 homers in a season since 1977. But Cecil Fielder smashed 51 four-baggers during the 1990 season! The 27-year-old fielder is the first baseman for the Detroit Tigers. He has both dingers (home runs) and fans a-plenty. His teammate Dave Bergman says, "The most important thing about Cecil is that he's nicer than he is big." (Cecil is 6 feet 3 and over 230 pounds.)

The 50 Club

Babe Ruth led the 50 Club, with four 50-plus-homer seasons. In 1927 Babe smashed 60 homers. Yankee Roger Maris belted 61 in 1961. Jimmie Foxx hit 58 in 1932 for the Philadelphia Athletics. In 1938 he hit 50 for the Boston Red Sox. Hank Greenberg of the Detroit Tigers bashed 58 in 1938. Hack Wilson hacked 56 for the Chicago Cubs in 1930. Ralph Kiner homered 54 times for the Pittsburgh Pirates in 1949 and hit 51 in 1947. Yankee slugger Mickey Mantle hit 54 in 1961 and 52 in 1956. Willie Mays hit 52 in 1965 for the San Francisco Giants and 51 in 1955 for the New York Giants. Johnny Mize hit 51 for the New York Giants in 1947 and Cecil Fielder hit 51 in 1990 for the Detroit Tigers.

Fifty is great, but 49 isn't bad. What about players who came close but couldn't quite get to number 50? As of 1990, here are the players who had 49 homers in a season:

Babe Ruth	New York Yankees	1930
Lou Gehrig	New York Yankees	1934
Lou Gehrig	New York Yankees	1936
Ted Kluszewski	Cincinnati Reds	1954
Willie Mays	San Francisco Giants	1962
Harmon Killebrew	Minnesota Twins	1964
Frank Robinson	Baltimore Orioles	1966
Harmon Killebrew	Minnesota Twins	1969
Andre Dawson	Chicago Cubs	1987
Mark McGwire	Oakland Athletics	1987

20-Victory Season

Star pitcher Dave Stewart of the Oakland Athletics finished the 1990 season saying, "I'm the best, period. Nothing else to say." That's because his 20-victory season marked only the tenth time since World War II that anyone has posted four consecutive 20-win seasons. The rest of the short list includes Hall of Famers Warren Spahn, Robin Roberts, Catfish Hunter, Jim Palmer (twice) and Juan Marichal. Also included are Ferguson Jenkins, Dave McNally and Wilbur Wood.

Dave Stewart

A Fan's Dream: Hanging Out with Idols

The first reason people are called fans is that "fan" spells out the first three letters in the word "fanatic." Thousands of people today are actually living the baseball fan's dream: a day in the life of a major-league star. The craze is called fantasy camp. All but four of the 26 major-league clubs take part in this business. Some camps, such as those run by the Dodgers and Mets, allow only about 100 fans. Some, like Baltimore's, take any number. Almost all camps are restricted to fans age 30 and older. The cost runs anywhere between $2,295 and $4,495. What does that buy? Fans stay, play and dine at spring training camps. They bring their own gloves, cleats and socks. They come home with goodies like personalized uniforms, bats, baseball cards and videos. They sometimes get sore muscles and bruised egos. But they always meet and get to know their favorite players!

Greg Meets Gregg

Greg Olson catches for the Atlanta Braves. Gregg Olson pitches for the Baltimore Orioles. The Braves catcher is constantly getting letters meant for the Oriole pitcher. He says, "How in the world can someone write a letter to an Orioles pitcher and send it to Atlanta? I have more Gregg Olson baseball cards [enclosed in the letters in hopes of being autographed and returned] than anyone in America."

Greg Olson met Gregg Olson at the 61st All-Star game. The meeting took place at a Wrigley Field workout in Chicago in July 1990. The Atlanta Olson told the Baltimore Olson that it had not been easy walking in the relief pitcher's shadow.

"Here are some of your baseball cards fans have sent me to sign," said Greg Olson. "They seldom ask me to sign my own."

The All-Star game is played annually between the best players of the National League and the best of the American League. Making the All-Star team was just a wild dream for Greg. It looked as if he would always be a career minor-leaguer. But he was in the right place at the right time. In 1990 a few releases and injuries to other players led him to the majors and the chance to be an All-Star. Now the Baltimore Olson says, "He's no longer in my shadow. He's an all-star on his own and I'm rootin' for him." Now the one piece of mail Greg Olson wouldn't mind getting is Gregg Olson's paycheck. Greg is paid the major-league minimum—$100,000. The Baltimore Olson gets $270,000.

It's a Whole New Ball Game

How different is 1990 baseball from 1950 baseball? Check out these official figures:

	1950	1990
Value of franchise (Dodgers)	$4.2 million	$225 million
Hot dog	$ .10	$2.50
Average ticket	$1.60	$8.00
Average player salary	$11,000	$600,000
Attendance per game	16,550	26,750
Big-League baseball	$2.80	$11.40
Pro model glove	$25	$250
Major-League revenues	$32.1 million	$1.3 billion

Baseball Timelines

1869: The Cincinnati Red Stockings become the first pro team in the United States. The highest-paid player receives $1,400 a year.

1903: The first World Series is played. The champions of the two major leagues meet in a best-of-nine series to win the title of world champion. The Boston Pilgrims (now the Red Sox) beat the Pittsburgh Pirates, five games to three.

1905: Frank Smith of the White Sox no-hits the Detroit Tigers, 15–0, the largest margin of victory ever in a no-hitter.

1911: The practice of honoring outstanding players begins when the makers of Chalmers automobiles give a car to the leading players in each league.

1918: Due to the war, major-league baseball ends its season a month early.

1919: On September 28 the New York Giants and the Philadelphia Phillies play the only game in this century that lasts less than one hour.

1922: George Sisler of the St. Louis Browns hits in 41 straight games. He would hold that record until 1941. Joe DiMaggio broke it with his 56-game hitting streak.

1923: Yankee Stadium is built. Babe Ruth hits the stadium's first home run.

1927: The Yankee lineup of 1927 becomes known as Murderers' Row, the greatest hitting team ever. The Yanks win 110 games, led by Babe Ruth's 60 home runs and Lou Gehrig's 47, at a time when home runs are fairly rare.

1931: The Most Valuable Player (MVP) award is instituted by the Baseball Writers Association.

1939: The Baseball Hall of Fame opens in Cooperstown, New York, on June 12, 1939.

The entrance to the Baseball Hall of Fame

1944: Joe Nuxhall becomes the youngest major-league player in history. He begins as a pitcher for Cincinnati on the day he is 15 years, 10 months and 11 days old.

1947: Ted Williams wins the Triple Crown—batting title, home-run title, and Runs-Batted-In (RBI) title—but does not steal a single base during the entire season.

1951: Topps begins printing baseball cards and later becomes the leader in the baseball-card business.

1957: Hank Aaron pounds out 44 homers and 132 RBIs to lead the then Milwaukee Braves to their first and only World Series victory.

1957: Ted Williams becomes baseball's first century man—the first player to be paid $100,000. His pay sets a salary milestone.

1957: Stan Musial sets the National League record for the longest span of time between first and last batting titles. Stan won his first title in 1943 and his last in 1957, 14 years later.

1957: The American League makes batting helmets mandatory.

1958: The Brooklyn Dodgers move to California and become the Los Angeles Dodgers.

1960: White Sox owner Bill Veeck is the first to put names on the backs of his players' uniforms.

1962: Maury Wills of the Los Angeles Dodgers steals 104 bases (in 165 games), breaking Ty Cobb's 1915 record of 96 bases (in 156 games).

1963: After 3,630 hits, Stan Musial, Cardinals number 6, calls it quits.

1964: On May 31 the New York Mets and the San Francisco Giants play the longest game ever in the major leagues. They play 23 innings. The doubleheader ends seven hours, 32 minutes after it begins.

1966: Frank Robinson becomes the only player voted the Most Valuable Player in both the National League and the American League. He won in 1961 playing for Cincinnati. Now he cops the MVP award again, playing in a different league for Baltimore.

1968 : Bobby Bonds becomes the only player in the 20th century to hit a grand-slam home run in his very first major-league game. He hits it for the San Francisco Giants on June 25, 1968.

1969: On August 5, visiting Pirates slugger Willie Stargell bats the only ball ever hit out of Dodger Stadium.

1969: Major-league baseball celebrates the game's centennial. Sportswriters and broadcasters name Joe DiMaggio the greatest living player and best center fielder in the history of the game.

1970: Ping! The aluminum bat is introduced in baseball.

1971: On September 17 all nine White Sox batters drive in a run as Chicago beats the California Angels, 9–4.

1980: George Brett is named the American League's MVP after batting .390. It is the highest average in the major leagues since 1941, when Ted Williams hit .406.

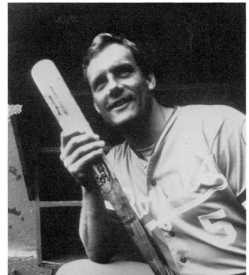

George Brett and the controversial pine-tar bat

1981: On June 12 the players go on strike for the second time in history and shut down the season for 50 days.

1982: Ricky Henderson swipes 130 bases.

1986: On September 29, for the first time in history, two brothers face each other as rookie starting pitchers. Greg Maddux of the Chicago Cubs beat older brother Mike of the Philadelphia Phillies, 8–3.

1987: Yankee hurler Phil Niekro retires at age 48, with 318 lifetime wins. The knuckleball specialist won a record 16 games in both 1984 and 1985.

1989: Wade Boggs of the Boston Red Sox becomes the first modern-day player to get 200 or more hits for seven straight years.

1989: On August 22 Nolan Ryan of the Texas Rangers fans Oakland's Rickey Henderson for his 5,000th career strikeout.

1989: As the San Francisco Giants and their neighbor, the Oakland Athletics, are about to start Game 3 of the World Series, an earthquake strikes California.

1990: On August 15 Mark McGwire of the Oakland Athletics hits a 10th-inning upper-deck grand slam against Boston. He becomes the first player ever to hit 30 or more homers in each of his first four seasons.

Index